Bilingual Edition

LET'S LOOK AT FEELINGS™

Edición Bilingüe

What I Look Like When I Am ⦿ Surprised ⦿

Cómo me veo cuando estoy ⦿ sorprendido ⦿

Joanne Shepherd
Traducción al español:
María Cristina Brusca

The Rosen Publishing Group's
PowerStart Press™ & **Editorial Buenas Letras**™
New York

1

Published in 2004 by The Rosen Publishing Group, Inc.
29 East 21st Street, New York, NY 10010

First Edition

Book Design: Kim Sonsky
Photo Credits: All photos by Maura B. McConnell.

Shepherd, Joanne
What I look like when I am surprised = Cómo me veo cuando estoy sorprendido / Joanne Shepherd ; translated by María Cristina Brusca.
p. cm. — (Let's look at feelings)
Includes bibliographical references and index.
Summary: This book describes what different parts of the face look like when a person is surprised.
ISBN 1-4042-7511-8
1. Surprise in children—Juvenile literature [1. Surprise 2. Facial expression 3. Emotions 4. Spanish language materials—Bilingual]   I. Title II. Title: Cómo me veo cuando estoy sorprendido   III. Series
BF723.S87 S4418 2004   2003-009147
152.4—dc21

Manufactured in the United States of America

Due to the changing nature of Internet links, PowerStart Press has developed an online list of Web sites related to the subject of this book. This site is updated regularly. Please use this link to access the list:

http://www.buenasletraslinks.com/llafe/sorprendido

Contents

Contenido

I am surprised.

Estoy sorprendida.

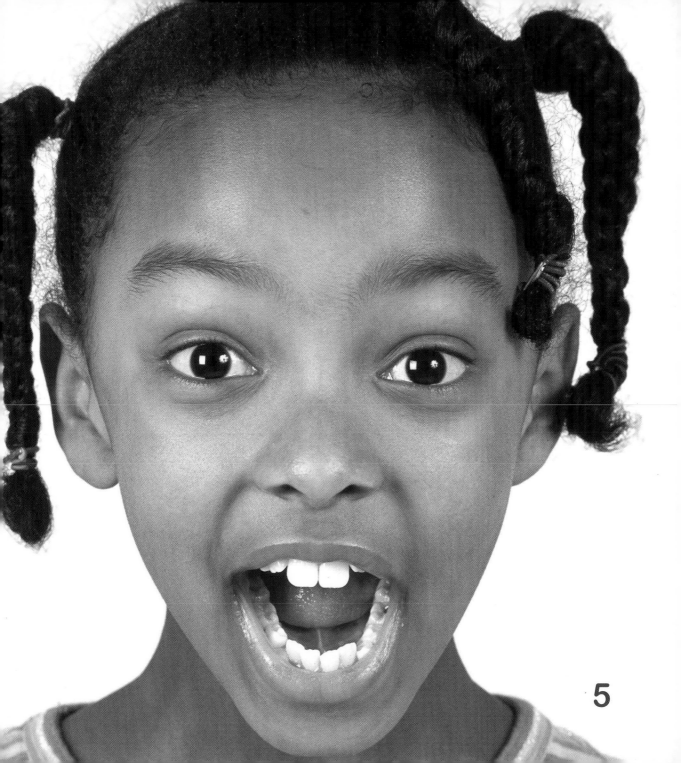

My eyebrows go up when I am surprised.

Cuando estoy sorprendido, mis cejas se levantan.

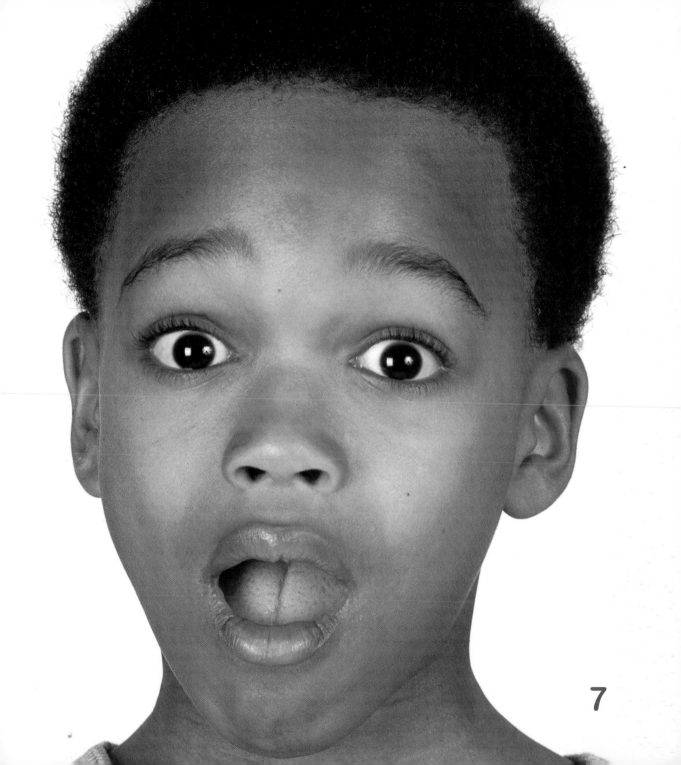

7

When I am surprised one eyebrow goes up and one goes down.

Cuando estoy sorprendido, una ceja se levanta y la otra se baja.

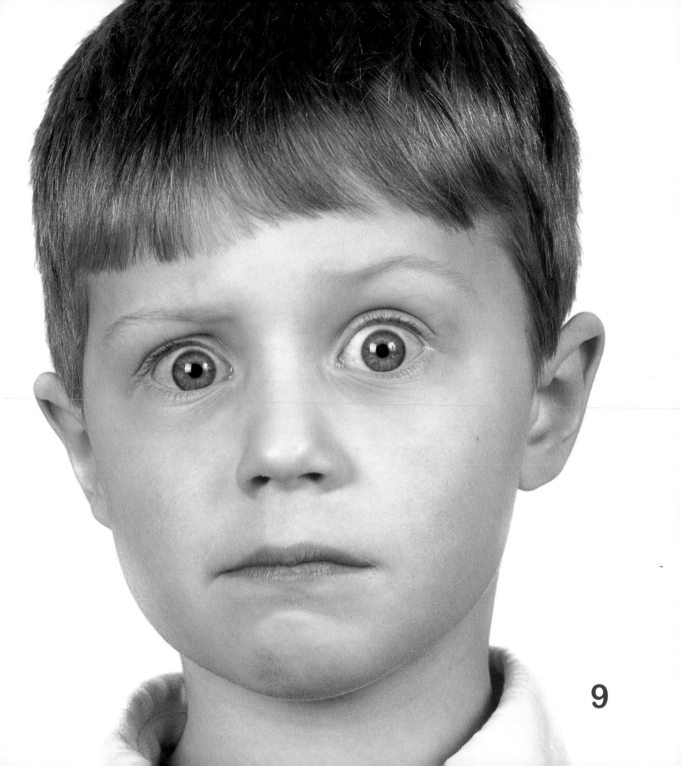

9

My mouth opens in a yell
when I am surprised.

Mi boca se abre en un grito,
cuando estoy sorprendido.

11

When I am surprised there are lines on each side of my mouth.

Cuando estoy sorprendido, se forman líneas a cada lado de mi boca.

13

When I am surprised my chin drops.

Cuando estoy sorprendido, mi mentón se baja.

15

You can see my teeth when
I am surprised.

Puedes ver mis dientes,
cuando estoy sorprendido.

17

My nostrils look bigger
when I am surprised.

Cuando estoy sorprendida,
las ventanas de mi nariz se
ven más grandes.

My cheeks are high and round when I am surprised.

Cuando estoy sorprendida, mis mejillas se ven más altas y redondas.

21

This is what I look like when I am surprised.

Así me veo cuando estoy sorprendido.

23

Words to Know
Palabras que debes saber

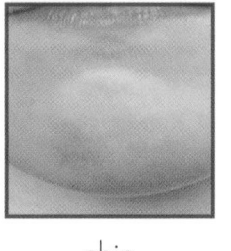

cheek
mejilla

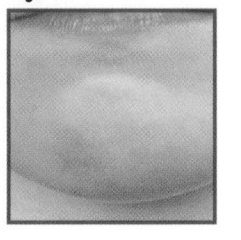

chin
mentón

eyebrow
ceja

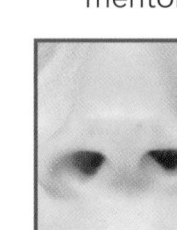

mouth
boca

nostrils
ventanas de la nariz

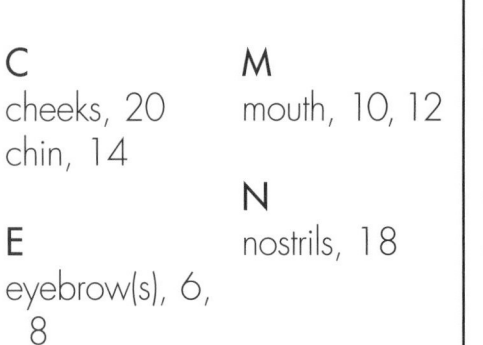

teeth
dientes